Field Trip!

Apple Orchard

Catherine Anderson

Heinemann Library
Chicago, Illinois

© 2005 Heinemann Library
a division of Reed Elsevier Inc.
Chicago, Illinois

Customer Service 888-454-2279
Visit our website at www.heinemannlibrary.com

Page layout by Kim Kovalick, Heinemann Library
Printed and bound in China by South China Printing Company Limited.
Photo research by Janet Lankford Moran

09 08 07 06 05
10 9 8 7 6 5 4 3 2 1

Library of Congress Cataloging-in-Publication Data
Anderson, Catherine, 1974-
  Apple orchard / Catherine Anderson.
     v. cm. -- (Field trip!)
  Contents: Where do apples come from? -- What is an apple orchard? -- When can you pick the apples? -- How do you pick the apples? -- What happens to the apples next? -- How do they make cider? -- Where do the apples and cider go? -- What can you find in the orchard store? -- What can you take home? -- Apple orchard map.
  ISBN 1-4034-6159-7 (HC), 1-4034-6166-X (Pbk.)
 1. Apples--Juvenile literature. 2. Orchards--Juvenile literature. [1. Apples. 2. Orchards.] I. Title. II. Series.
  SB363.A63 2004
  634'.11--dc22

                                    2003027857

Acknowledgments
The author and publishers are grateful to the following for permission to reproduce copyright material:
p. 4, 5l, 6, 7, 8, 10, 11, 12, 13, 14, 15, 16, 18, 19, 20, 21, back cover Warling Studios/Heinemann Library; p. 5r Janet Moran/Heinemann Library; p. 9 Mark E. Gibson/Corbis; p. 17 Greg Williams/Heinemann Library ; p. 23 (T-B) Warling Studios/Heinemann Library, Warling Studios/Heinemann Library, Janet Moran/Heinemann Library, Warling Studios/Heinemann Library

Cover photograph by Warling Studios/Heinemann Library

Every effort has been made to contact copyright holders of any material reproduced in this book. Any omissions will be rectified in subsequent printings if notice is given to the publisher.

Special thanks to the Jacobsons at The Apple Barn in Elkhorn, Wisconsin, for their help in the preparation of this book.

Special thanks to our advisory panel for their help in the preparation of this series:

Alice Bethke
Library Consultant
Palo Alto, California

Malena Bisanti-Wall
Media Specialist
American Heritage Academy
Canton, Georgia

Ellen Dolmetsch, MLS
Tower Hill School
Wilmington, Delaware

Contents

Where Do Apples Come From? 4

What Is an Apple Orchard? 6

When Can You Pick the Apples? 8

How Do You Pick the Apples? 10

What Happens to the Apples Next? . . . 12

How Do They Make Cider? 14

Where Do the Apples and Cider Go? . . . 16

What Can You Find in the
     Orchard Store? 18

What Can You Take Home? 20

Apple Orchard Map 22

Picture Glossary 23

Note to Parents and Teachers 24

Index 24

Some words are shown in bold, **like this.**
You can find them in the picture glossary on page 23.

Where Do Apples Come From?

Apples grow on apple trees.

Apples are the **fruit** of the apple tree.

Apple trees start as tiny **seeds.**

The trees grow big and make apples.

What Is an Apple Orchard?

An apple orchard has many apple trees.

There may be different kinds of apple trees there.

You can go to an apple orchard to buy apples.

You can buy other things made with apples there, too.

When Can You Pick the Apples?

Apples are ready to be picked in the fall.

Then, the trees are full of ripe apples.

The orchard workers pick the apples.

You may be able to pick some, too.

How Do You Pick the Apples?

Lift an apple and carefully twist it off the branch.

Put your apples in a **bushel.**

Orchard workers use tall ladders to reach the tops of trees.

They put the apples in bags that they carry.

What Happens to the Apples Next?

You can wash the apples and eat them.

You can take some home to make apple pies or applesauce.

The orchard workers take the other apples to the barn.

There, they sort them and put them in bags.

How Do They Make Cider?

Some apples are squished to make cider.

This machine squeezes the juice out of apples.

tank

jug

The cider goes into big tanks.

The orchard workers fill jugs with cider.

Where Do the Apples and Cider Go?

Cider and fresh apples go into a cooler.

The cooler keeps them cool and fresh.

Some of the cider and apples are sold at the orchard.

Some go to stores to be sold.

What Can You Find in the Orchard Store?

apple syrup | caramel apple | apple pie

The orchard store sells many things made from apples.

They have apple pies, apple **syrup,** and caramel apples.

Some orchards have a kitchen to make pies.

You can get one hot from the oven!

What Can You Take Home?

You can take home the apples that you picked.

You can buy other things from the store.

You give your money to the store clerk.

See you again soon!

Apple Orchard Map

apple orchard

kitchen

barn

cooler

orchard store

Picture Glossary

 **bushel**
page 10
kind of container

 **fruit**
page 4
part of a plant that holds
the seeds

 **seed**
page 5
small resting plant that can grow
into a big plant

 **syrup**
page 18
sweet liquid for pouring on foods

Note to Parents and Teachers

Reading for information is an important part of a child's literacy development. Learning begins with a question about something. Help children think of themselves as investigators and researchers by encouraging their questions about the world around them. Each chapter in this book begins with a question. Read the question together. Look at the pictures. Talk about what you think the answer might be. Then read the text to find out if your predictions were correct. Think of other questions you could ask about the topic, and discuss where you might find the answers. Assist children in using the picture glossary and the index to practice new vocabulary and research skills.

Index

apple pies 12, 18, 19

applesauce. 12

apple syrup 18

apple trees 4, 5, 6, 8, 11

bagging 13

bags 11, 13

bushel. 10

caramel apples 18

cider 14–15, 16, 17

clerk. 21

cooler. 16

fall 8

jugs 15

ladders 11

orchard store 18–19, 20–21

orchard workers. . . . 9, 11, 13, 15

picking. 8–9, 10–11

seeds 5

sorting 13

stores 17, 18, 20

tanks 15